'MUMALITY'
My reality of being a mum!

©
All rights reserved
April 2023
Nottinghamshire
Written by Melissa Fae Wardman
Edited by Stewart King

This book goes out to all my fellow mums, mum's to be or fathers and even if you are feeling it right now, I promise you are not alone. I hear you loud and clear!

I'm Melissa and this is mine and my husband's journey within the first year or so of being a mummy and daddy to our little girl Ivy.

I'm here to tell you my raw story and openly admit it isn't all sunshine and rainbows. In fact I'm here to explain the literal shit storm of events that can happen. Yet I wouldn't have it any other way.

One thing I would like to say is that before welcoming our beautiful girl into the world, I have always suffered from anxiety for as long as I can remember. So having Ivy definitely heightened the anxiety. This was a blessing in a weird way though, because it then meant I seeked help to heal and be the strongest mum I could be. Which then meant I could write this book and hopefully help others!

I am dedicating this book to my beautiful girl and my soulmate husband, Team Wardman!

Hopefully you will enjoy reading this book as much as I have had writing it.

Melissa ♥

The greater your storm, the brighter your rainbow.

CONTENTS

1. 'Fourth Trimester' Coming home (10)
2. 'Fourth Trimester' I wasn't ready (16)
3. 'Fourth Trimester' Not in control (22)
4. Bonding (28)
5. Paternity End (34)
6. Finding my feet (40)
7. Fast changes (46)
8. New to parent life (50)
9. Reflux #Nightmare (56)
10. Weaning (60)
11. Crawling (66)
12. Teething (70)
13. High temperature and febrile fits (74)
14. Holiday with a baby/toddler (84)
15. Sleep regressions and night terrors (92)
16. First birthday party and the future (100)

Chapter One

'Fourth Trimester', Coming home

Ahhh the 'fourth trimester'...

The one no one prepares you for, in fact from my experience the one no one bloody talks about! It's a thing, a real thing and I'm telling you now mummy whatever you are feeling, or may feel within this phase ***it's normal.***

If it wasn't for me having the most amazing support from my close family I honestly don't know how I would have coped! That being said, it is also normal to sail through and not experience any of the things I did and for that I envy. When you hear about other ladies experiencing baby blues or postnatal you never really think it's going to be you. I mean you're happy and it's what you've planned for so why would you feel that way? I was naive really, I was too much in a pregnant love bubble to even dream that I wouldn't feel the sudden gush of love. Of course I was scared for the change but I really thought I had my shit together.

So after 9 months of constant baby bump attention, doors being opened, cups of tea on tap from my hubby and basically feeling like a queen for just under a year.

BOOM it wasn't all about me anymore!

The human I was growing was no longer part of *my* human. I wasn't ready for it but at the same time I was...

At least I thought I was, How confusing!

Due to taking certain anxiety medication I had to stay in hospital for two days with Ivy. It was perfect and even now I will say I smashed it! I was in this lovely little bubble, just me and my little baby girl. Of course I missed Mat but I had a tiny human to focus on and those two days will always be such precious memories to me, just before reality hit! Or shall we say hormones hit!

The last day before leaving the hospital my sister Kyle rang to congratulate me but also explained I may find the next few days hard and if I do it's okay and that she's only a text away. Unlucky for her but lucky (weirdly) for me she had struggled herself as a new mum and was very switched on to how post baby can affect mums mentally. Later that evening I was discharged and of course we did the whole photo of baby daddy walking proudly with baby in the car seat.

Funny story - Ivy made a groan noise all the way home that sounded like a squeaky door constantly being opened and I really thought that I had brought home something possessed, I wanted a refund haha!

Back home, my mum was waiting with my brother and sister in law excited to meet her grandchild for the first time! As soon as I walked through the door I saw the pram and moses basket waiting for **my baby** because **I'm a mum**. I felt sick and a sudden emotion rushed over me. I didn't say anything, I just wished for everyone to leave so I could let it out. My mum knows me so well and she knew I wasn't right, she was also prepared for me to feel this way with previous anxiety episodes so she hung around.

As soon as my brother left, I broke down saying *'what have I done mum, I'm so scared'* I just couldn't understand that something I loved so much whilst she was still in my belly and I was so excited to meet, that I suddenly wanted it all to go away. I didn't want this life, I wanted just me and Mat again. My mum sat with me and explained that it's short term feelings and it's all down to hormones. Let me tell you those pesky hormones have a lot to answer for! I was so scared for my mum to leave us (brand new parents alone, with no midwife or red buzzer!) She reassured me we would all be fine and she was only a phone call away.

That night I set my alarm every two hours to feed Ivy, as I was so scared to miss her feeding cues or I was scared I wouldn't wake at all! Everything I had done the past two days went out the window. I was a hormonal, anxious mess. We had about five hours of broken sleep that night, but we did it together. In the morning when she woke she started to make a weird noise. I quickly whipped her out of the moses basket, shouting for Mat and asking him what was happening, not that he had a flaming clue either! lots of white stuff came out of her nose. I rang the birthing unit crying,
saying my baby couldn't breathe! They calmed me down and explained that all It was, was mucus and that Ivy was perfectly fine! It's something babies can bring up after being birthed.

Looking back I feel silly for this now, but how was I to know? At this point I really wish I had done more research on the 'fourth trimester!'

After getting over that episode I rang mum asking when she would be able to see us. I can remember physically shaking, holding the phone as I was absolutely terrified of something bad happening to Ivy. I would say from this day on I think my mum and step dad practically lived with us for at least a month! There weren't many days when they didnt come and have tea with us. My mum didn't leave mine or Mats' side, she helped with daily chores and Ivy but mainly with me, she was there for the 10 million meltdowns that I had everyday.

It's so true when they say no matter how old you are you still need your mum. She helped *me* grow as a mum, taking the baby steps with me. She understood It was something I needed support with and for that I'm forever grateful because I understand not everyone has that kind of support. Throughout this time no one else mattered to me as long as I had my support bubble of family and friends around me and Ivy was safe, everyone else outside of my bubble didn't exist.

As awful as it sounds, the real world felt so far away and meant nothing to me. People's birthdays could come and go or lovely events could happen but for me it didn't feel as though I could acknowledge that they were happening when I had something ***so big*** that was happening to me. The change hit me hard. When I look back now I have so much guilt, as I would do anything to relive those first few months differently and to enjoy every moment but sadly baby blues and postnatal is a real thing which can make something so beautiful feel like a trauma.

Chater Two

'Fourth Trimester' I wasn't ready

Many people said to me and will say to you *"Don't let anyone come round to visit for the first week, settle with just you and your family"*. This is true, so so true! Did I listen? No? Should I have listened? ABSOLUTELY BLOOMING YES!l

Mat's family *(seven people to be exact)* came to visit Ivy, the day after I had come home. This was day three post baby, which is usually when hormones are starting to drop and this is when they are revving up getting ready to have an after party in your brain, playing havoc with your emotions! As well as seven of Mat's family visiting, I already had mum and Colin *(my step dad)* at our house and also my cousin Laura and her hubby Stew! (these two are also myself and Mat's besties). They were all so excited to meet and hold the new addition and to make it easy for everyone a huge chippy takeaway was bought and shared between us all. I know that sounds lovely and you know what, it was! For everyone but me.

I sat watching everyone, with no appetite, stitches down below and what I now know was mastitis. Why were they all so happy, why did I feel so scared and lonely? Lots of photos were taken that day and honestly, I hate them all. I look so broken and Ill.

I didn't have time to take on board the massive change in my life and to me, everyone was going about their day like it was nothing.

The thing I found the hardest was, before birth I had everyone asking how I was feeling and if 'bump' was ok. Now it wasn't about me anymore. Everyone wants to meet and hold our baby. Yet I wasn't ok. Again this was hormones (I told you they were pesky) and I love everyone who visited dearly. But in the midst of things it was hard and I've said it over and over to many people that I wish I could now revisit these times with the mind I have today.

Having people come round to visit Ivy was hard and it wasn't because I didn't want anyone to hold her, it was because I felt so broken. I couldn't bear letting anyone else see how much I was struggling. As well as not wanting to leave Ivy's side I also didn't want to reply to anyone via text or phone call. If I did speak to them I felt like they would know I was struggling and I would have to admit those feelings.

There was a part of me that felt as if I was failing. I said many times to Laura that I feel as if I don't deserve Ivy because she's so perfect and everything I want, yet my mind won't let the changes in. I always loved her from <u>day one</u> and having her in our lives was never the problem, I was just creating a barrier in my mind. If I was numb to everything 'baby' then maybe I could be numb to the feelings I was currently battling with. It will always be the hardest thing to explain because even
 I struggled to understand my emotions at the time. I will always find comfort after speaking to many people how normal it actually is. When I look at Ivy now it hurts me that's how I felt. How could I let myself feel all these things and be numb towards my little munchkin?

Truthfully I never let myself feel good or bad feelings, I was in a new mum bubble that just needed to grow a little bigger before it eventually popped.

I can now say that I am so proud, looking back because I still achieved when I was at my lowest. I was still a mum, just with some help. I didn't give up altogether and she was still a happy healthy baby.

Chapter Three

'Fourth Trimester' Not in control

Not only were my hormones doing the dirty on me, making me have night sweats like you wouldn't believe *(Honestly for the first week I would wake up saturated and every time I would check if I had wet myself, crazy!)* but I was also healing from labour.

Although I had a pretty straight forward labour, I tore quite badly when pushing out my little melon. This caused me to have stitches in three places. I was struggling to wee without it stinging and to sit down. No matter how I sat I wasn't comfortable. As well as being in pain down below, I was in agony with my boobs and also my under arms. Day three and four my boobs grew and grew to the point where they looked like they would pop (Dolly Parton vibes!) and my under arms were just as bad, it looked like I had three golf balls under my armpits, I couldn't put my arms down comfortably. So to add to the stress of a newborn, hormonal baby blues and a car crash down below I decided it was best to get it checked out.

They saw me that day back on the ward, where several doctors had a look and more importantly saw my boobs in my grandma's bra! Yes, true story my boobs went so big I couldn't fit into mine or my mum's bras so I had to wear my darling grandma's non wired cone shaped bra. I had mastitis that was caused from a backlog of milk which backed up into my glands under my arms. For this I needed antibiotics which were usually given by IV in hospital. I broke down and explained how I'm struggling to bond with my baby and being away from her is going to make things even harder.

I also had serious guilt for leaving Mat with her. The doctor agreed he would discharge me with oral antibiotics but if I started with a temperature to come straight back. It was at that moment I realised I had admitted I was struggling to bond with Ivy and In some ways it then gave me the confidence to speak out loud at home about it. When I came home I explained how I was feeling to Mat and my mum but they already knew, they could see, it was obvious.

Of all the people helping me through this tough time, my cousin/bestie Laura is everything a girl wishes for in a friend. Who else would lie next to me in the early hours of the morning to try and help me get some sleep, in between mild contractions whilst Mat slept.

Funny story - a memory for us was when I said a contraction was coming on and BOOM the biggest fart came out and definitely went on for at least 5 seconds. Evidently now, the baby pushes on everything including your little trump bubbles! I love this girl though, it literally is a friendship through thick and thin

She was with me right until I went into the hospital to give birth and she was there as soon as I got home.
I would like to say it was all a lovely baby bubble for her but she was straight in the deep end consoling me whilst holding hot and cold flannels on my extremely enlarged breasts whilst I sobbed in the bath. She and Stew were at our house
everyday for a while with my mum, supporting me and Mat.

We had the strongest, most loving support bubble.
I see positives now, but at the time it was a challenging

situation. I felt so alone but now Ivy has the most amazing bond with all these people, she never feels alone and for that it was worthwhile feeling that way.

The mastitis had caused my boobs to swell so much that they looked like they were going to pop. Luckily the hospital wanted to keep an eye on me so I went in. When I got there the midwife advised that while I was waiting for the antibiotics to kick in, that (if I could) I needed to express some milk to ease the pain.

Story time again - We had a weird moment where I had to hold a sick bowl whilst she hand expressed my boobs. I know this is a natural thing but at this time, my life was just getting more crazy by the minute, especially when my milk hit her in the uniform with pressure I've only ever seen when Mat jet washes the car!

She said if I struggled hand expressing, I'd have to try and pump if I could afford a machine or know anyone with one. As doing this would stop the infection getting worse. WELL what another experience.
 But one I needed for a good old giggle. Luckily, Laura had a pumping machine that I could use but pumping is something I never wanted to do. I admire and love the fact women can breastfeed and it's the most natural thing ever! But I never wanted to and couldn't bring myself to do it, which again ladies is also perfectly fine, do not let anyone make you feel bad for this, you do what is right for you and your baby.
So there I sat on the edge of my bed in massive knickers with a brick for a sanitary towel and my boobs like two boulders out in the open for everyone to see. Laura and mum get the machine out of the box and set it up.

Believe it or not me, mum and Laura all hadn't breastfed before so we had never used a machine and clearly didn't read the instructions. I held it to my boobs and Laura clicked, which we now know was the WRONG button. Talk about the speed! My poor nipples were going for it which seemed like the speed of light! Honestly ladies, I never knew your nipples could stretch that far! Hats off to my breastfeeding mummies as I'm scarred for life. *"No no no no no no, stop no stop this isn't for me"* I cried. We all giggled and couldn't believe this is how we were spending our Sunday afternoon. Laura stood up and said *"Well back to the hot and cold flannels we go"* they didn't care, we all didn't care. They just wanted to support me and literally did whatever it took to help make it a little easier.

Meanwhile whilst this is going off Mat is holding the fort with Stew (bless them) downstairs with a newborn and took it all in his stride, he did everything he could whether it meant feeds in the night, even if he was up for work in a few hours or just sending me to bed to catch up on sleep. We are each other's world and will do anything to stop each other from hurting. I know that I'm extremely lucky to have this and trust me I don't let him forget what he means to me.

Chapter Four

Bonding

For the first week of being home I spent the whole time crying throughout the day, living on a pack of biscuits and pacing floors. I couldn't settle, my world was upside down. I was so angry at myself that something so amazing was causing me to feel the way I did. I knew I loved her, I couldn't be away from her! When I showered or was upstairs I would shout downstairs to ask if she was ok constantly. Yet when I was with her I felt nothing, or at least I thought I didn't.

Sooner than me holding her, changing her or even pushing the pram I would have easily let my mum and Mat take over every time. I know to some people this may all seem awful but it's real, real feelings and real life. It is so much more common than I thought. In fact most mums that I spoke to had gone through the same or something similar.

Kylie was a rock to me through all of this. I texted her a couple of days after being home saying *'I can't do this'* and she came round without me even having to ask. She spent a lot of days reassuring me and telling stories of her experiences with her daughter. Whilst she was with me I felt normal, I wasn't alone and finally someone understood this circus going off in my head.

She was my sunshine on a rainy day and for that I couldn't thank her enough. She supported me more than she will ever know.

I had always been told horror stories about health visitors but mine from our first conversation gave me hope. She came around on day five to weigh and check Ivy over. The minute she asked me if I was ok I broke down telling her how scared I was that I would never bond with Ivy. She turned to me and said *'Melissa although she Is your baby, she is a stranger to you and this world. You can't expect to feel a sudden rush of love for a stranger'* this was so true and so right, it was baby steps.

We spoke about ways to bond and from then she rang me a couple of times a week and visited every other week. Each time she visited I felt more love between me and Ivy, she reminded me how far I had come and I was starting to see it myself. Don't get me wrong I was still majorly overwhelmed and was still having a daily cry, but that's how I coped.

A couple of weeks into parent life I woke up and it was there, something clicked. I felt happiness and love towards Ivy. I mean overtime with the help of everyone around me it built up but I think I just realised that morning. I can remember like it was yesterday, my mum was outside pegging the washing out, watching us through the patio doors, I was laying on the play mat with Ivy holding her tiny hand and tears started streaming. My mum came in and smiled.
She knew it was finally happy tears. So bonding for me had finally started. I could start to enjoy time with me and Ivy.

Another thing my health visitor said to me was that babies do not realise they are no longer part of the mum's body and still think you are one person so that's why they usually cry for a cuddle.

This melted me, this tiny human just wanted love.

I must admit I found night feeds hard as I've never been good on zero sleep but giving cuddles with a bottle every two hours knowing that's all my little baby needs to feel safe and content made it a whole lot easier. I wish I could go back just one more time to a night feed! I never thought I would say that.

Speaking of night feeds, after the first night when Ivy brought up mucus, although I knew she was fine and it was normal, it scared me. To the point I couldn't sleep in our bed with the moses basket next to us. I know this sounds crazy but it was because it was higher than our bed so I could see her if I opened my eyes, I would have to sit up. In the daytime I realised our sofa was the same height as the moses basket. So what did we do? Sofa camp out!
It sounds crazy but I felt safe and Mat just wanted me to be happy. Honestly that guy would camp in the toilet with me if it meant I was happy, he truly is one in a million. Afterall it resulted in binge watching the whole of Benidorm! Night Sweats, night feeds, sofa camping and Benidorm, WILD!

Chapter Five

Paternity End

The two weeks of Mats paternity flew by, as expected I found it hard with him returning back to work. He was my safety blanket and the only bit of normality I had. Although I was a little more stronger in myself, I still didn't feel ready. There was also a side of me that felt massive guilt. I felt as if Mat had two weeks off, juggling a newborn and his wife. When I look back now he didn't stop, he was bouncing between us both making sure we were both ok whilst not knowing what the hell he was doing and still smashing being a new dad. He really is one of a kind and my soulmate.

One time that will always stay with me was when we visited the pub one afternoon with my mum and sister. It's just down the road from our house and it did me good to get out of my 'comfort zone'. Whilst we were there I was so scared to do anything, such as feed Ivy and when It came to changing her nappy there was no way. This is how it got to me, small things, but big to me. I can remember watching him walk off holding Ivy in one arm and the baby bag in another, realising how lucky I was, wishing I could just go and do that.

If it meant him doing something to make it easier on me he would, he wanted me to feel confident and ready.

As time went on we did it together, he would come in the toilet with me and support me. I honestly don't know what I was scared of, I had changed lots of my nieces and nephews nappies in the past but I guess hormones and anxiety wanted to make that hard for me too! Nowadays It's like having a rugby scrum with Ivy when changing her nappy.

Toddlers just want to make every little thing a challenge and let me tell you, I bloody feel like I've broken a sweat and completed a Ninja Warrior course when I've finally changed it!

I guess it was just as hard on Mat going back to work. Not only was he going to miss Ivy trillions but he also was worried about how I would cope. He felt comfort knowing that my mum would be around whenever I needed her. We would facetime many times a day and when he was on the nightshift my mum would even come stay a few nights and do the night feeds with me!

Again we made so many memories, it was like a girly sleepover mid week, only no alcohol but murder documentaries, chocolate and cups of tea at 3am. My mum would always say *'well we might as well, now we are up'* That woman is crazy though, there's been plenty of times she's put the washing in or done the pots early hours of the morning. Absolute machine.

I appreciate everything that my mum and Colin did for me.

I would treat her as much as I could, because I knew it was a big change for her as well, all of a sudden having to spend so much time at our house. She always says that she wouldn't have it any other way, but still I wanted to treat her!

I would buy us matching PJs for our sleepovers and have homemade cakes made for the night feeds (sugar was needed!) I had family with me all the time, which I know seems a little over the top but Mat felt more content knowing he could leave and not worry about me. Most of all so many good memories were made that we will cherish forever, not everyone gets to experience that. Silver lining and all.

Slowly as time went on my confidence grew and I told myself that I'm now not alone as I have Ivy! A little best friend to keep me company whilst Mat was working. Mum would ask me *'do you need me tonight?'* and I would say *'No but keep your phone right next to you!'*

Chapter Six

Finding my feet#

♥

With Mat being back at work things were still a little challenging. However with support from the health visitor and family members, I was starting to slowly find little strengths within motherhood.

Ivy was just over 3 weeks old and our friends came to visit who were expecting their baby boy. I sat there confidently explaining my experiences and letting them know if they feel the way I do (as men can feel it too) then it's completely normal and they are not alone. This was massive, I was supporting people through my experiences!

A week later I received a text to say they were having a few "wobbles" and weirdly it felt nice being able to support them.

For two reasons. Firstly, I understood what they were feeling, so I could help and secondly I felt NORMAL! I didn't feel alone but also it made me realise how far I had already come.

Fast forward a few months and one of Mats friends had a little baby boy, he messaged Mat to say how his missus was struggling. I had previously seen a video of her arriving home with her son and I could tell just from the video how she was feeling with the overwhelmed look on her face.

I had never even met her but I couldn't bear the thought of someone else feeling the way I did and feeling alone so I took it upon myself to message her and ask if she was up for visitors. She said that she was, so I told her I was coming round because I understood what she was going through. To be honest I feel like it was meant to be, we didn't want to see anyone else because of how we were feeling but we both agreed to meet, even though we didn't know each other.

That evening I popped round to her house for a cuppa, we spent a few hours chatting away, laughing and having a cry. We clicked instantly and I am forever grateful for meeting my girl Beth.

It just felt good being able to connect and have someone else that felt exactly how I did and we could even laugh about it! One thing that stays with me was when she stood up looking over her baby in the Moses basket and said *"you see I know I love him Liss but.."* and I said *"you don't need to explain babe, I understand and it's ok to feel that way"*.

From then on we were friends forever, from coffee dates to ranting to each other over Snapchat, picking the same pizza topping and having the same skin condition (yes haha! We won't get into that).
Sometimes I feel things really do happen for a reason.

As my maternity was through lockdown and covid times, it was really hard to find things which were still running, such as baby groups or swimming. So I improvised at home.
 I spent so much time printing monochrome pictures off for baby sensory or laying on foil mats looking up at projectors shining on the ceiling with Ivy. If anything, it helped me

keep busy throughout the day and without even realising, it kept me and Ivy bonding.

I just wanted the best for her, I would compare myself to other mums on Instagram all the time (I mean I still do) and I always felt that I wasn't doing enough.

Yet the reality is all mums lay on foil mats with their babies, staring up at the ceiling thinking is this enough? At the end of the day, until your baby is on the move, it's a potato, a cute one though, a sweet potato haha!

I was still at the stage where I found things hard though. Such as going out and not wanting to change her nappy, there were a few times where I didn't have a choice but to do it because I was on my own and after doing it I felt proud like I had achieved something. It sounds so silly but the little things for me were big achievements and I promise you baby steps are better than nothing at all. At the end of the day it's all new, we are overwhelmed, a little lost, learning as we go and bloody knackered!

So even if we learn little by little each day, It's enough.

I think at this point it is when my addiction to coffee started, so much so that I'm now a Barista haha. Honestly that's what I did most days with my mum or Mat, we would go out to a coffee shop, sit and have a drink. I would feed Ivy and try to feel abit of normality around me.
Although all these coffee dates and little walks around our estate were just small things and to some people would be easy to forget. To me it was *my* life and it was a huge

challenge that I was trying to overcome, things I couldn't do alone. I have never been someone that can be alone, I don't think I ever will be but I needed my close people more than ever around these times.

I found a love for taking photos of Ivy each day. I got her ready in a cute little outfit for the day and then took a quick snap. I then edited them on a software called Lightroom which changed the colours to make them look more professional. On Instagram I started to have a few little small businesses ask if Ivy would like to be a brand rep for them.

This was perfect as it was something I loved doing, capturing my little girl looking all cute and it kept me busy and again kept me bonding with her! It seems crazy really that taking photos would help me bond doesn't it? I would always write down her milestones on a pegboard to have in the photos with her or put nice things on crates in the background and this secretly
forced me to be with her and I fell in love more and more each day.

Chapter Seven

Fast Changes

♥

So for someone that has anxiety, I will tell you something that I wasn't prepared for: the amount of change! Change in routine, milk ounces and poo colour! I'm someone that usually sticks to routine in day to day life but this baby stuff is totally out of your hands and then once you feel like you've got a grip on it, boom! CHANGE AGAIN. As bad as this sounds though, it's really not too bad. It's just your baby changing, growing and developing but it does keep you on your toes.

Lets talk poo, yes poo. It's not something you really think about too much when it's just yourself but when you're changing a nappy frequently you soon start to take note of the colour, texture and even smell. It's crazy how within the first week, the colour change your baby's poo goes through from black tar on the first poo to chicken korma colour with bits in. I never knew if each change was normal and spent so much time googling and ringing the health visitor.
Looking back it was just because I cared, it wasn't Ivy I was struggling to bond with, it was me adapting to new life. I couldn't just sit down and switch off when I wanted to or go out and shop for pointless stuff. My life had changed completely, nothing was the same anymore and I'll be honest there have been plenty of times where it has gotten hard and I just wished for my old life back.

There isn't one mum I've spoken to yet that has not also felt the same thing, we get exhausted mentally and physically, it's so easy to have these thoughts cross your mind.

Now nearly two years on though, as lovely as it would be to sit and binge watch TV, get up when we want to and eat a meal out without a toddler hanging off your knee.

Me and Mat really wouldn't choose that now (honest truth) life would be so boring and samey. It's so true when they say something can be a beautiful nightmare, Ivy is the most testing little human being but hearing her laugh just makes all the hard times go away. She now makes us binge watch Peppa Pig, eat wooden fruit that she's 'cooked' in her play kitchen and dress up as bunnies. Now that's more entertaining than a Chinese takeaway on a Saturday night.

What I'm trying to say is, it's hard, my God one of the hardest things you will ever take on but it's the most rewarding, beautiful journey and it's all worth it.

Chapter Eight

New to the parent life

♥

As new parents we were both like two naive school kids going up to big school with no clue what was about to hit us in the new big wide world. What I mean by that is the silly little things you think you are doing perfectly right but in fact it's the total opposite, so let me talk you through these things to save you from making the same mistake!

- Milk tins! So not only is it hard enough being sleep deprived trying to count the scoops of milk needed for the bottles but it's also hard when you didn't know that a butter knife was not needed to level it off! You can use the side of the tin guys! In fact some even have a little bit sticking out to do this on. My cousin FaceTimed me and I propped her up whilst filling up milk pods for the day, she burst out laughing asking me what the hell I was doing. She said *'remove the foil fully and the metal ledge you can see sticking out, that's for levelling'* thanks Lilly.

- Zip baby grows! Buy these! Like right now. I promise you when it's 2am and your eyes are like piss holes in the snow and you are literally struggling to function, the last thing you want to be doing is lining up the buttons on a babygrow. Then as time goes on, the baby will start rolling during a nappy change, *zip!* easy as that. THEN the baby will literally turn into a piece of flat MDF when being changed, *zip!* happy mum, happy life. Lastly when the baby is no longer a baby and now requires on the move nappy changes BOOM! Zip sleepsuits.

- Food shopping on your own! One thing I struggled with was simply going out on my own, never mind going *food shopping* on my own. The thing is, it wasn't even the pram that was the problem because Ivy would sleep or just lay there whilst I pushed her around at this stage, it was the predicament on where to put the food. I spent many times carrying a basket in one hand whilst pushing the pram with the other. Or shoving all the goods under the pram and having massive anxiety the whole way round the shop thinking I was being watched on CCTV in case I was stealing. One day I came out of the shop (struggling) to see another mum put the car seat in the trolley. I thought *'well blow me down, two birds with one stone!'* Obviously as you're all probably aware that would only be ok for a short period of time, due to not keeping babies in car seats for too long. However I figured that my pram carrycot, once taken off the frame would fit perfectly in a big trolley! Of Course I couldn't fit much shopping in so I would then sometimes have to brave the communal trolley with the plastic baby chair attached to the top (which Ivy hated so that wasn't very often!) But if you do use that, take a blanket to cover it over first, I think Ivy found it uncomfortable but that definitely helped. This was another massive anxiety of mine though. It took me ages to build the confidence to do because I really couldn't see how I could make it work. Then one day I thought *'what have I got to lose?'* I couldn't just wait on fresh food around Mat's shifts. So I prepared the bag with a spare bottle and a dummy.

51

- Fed her and got myself out of the house as quickly as I could whilst I still had it in my head that I could do it.

- The blue line on the nappy! Now this is something I knew prior to Having Ivy, but I found that it was something many family members didn't know when looking after her. It's basically a line through the nappy that changes to blue when the baby has done a wee. It sounds obvious but when your baby is crying at 3am ,it really does help! Or if your baby is anything like Ivy she didn't like to have a wet nappy at all. When she was unsettled it was a good indicator. I mean it wasn't always the case of a wet nappy but it really did help from time to time. Oh and also don't forget to pull the frills out from around the legs of the nappy! This 100% prevents leakage.

Ain't no hood

like

MOTHERHOOD!

Chapter Nine

Reflux #Nightmare

♥

Now if you're one of the unlucky parents to be blessed with a baby that has reflux, I feel you!
Wouldn't it be perfect to just feed your baby to sleep and have a lovely little cuddle after? Or to have any kind of floor time with the baby gym or tummy time roller without a sick surprise. You can never have too many muslin cloths, we literally had at least 20 as we could get through as many as five a day and we still use them now.

The positive thing was it never really bothered Ivy when she was sick. She was oblivious and usually I wouldn't notice straight away if she was rolling around, bless her it still gives me mum guilt now. It's just the constant sicky clothes, bibs and also the change of your own clothes! It did get to the point where the odd time she would drink her bottle and after a burp she would bring the whole thing back up even if we stopped many times throughout the feed for a burp. It didn't matter what we did differently, she was still sick and the smell of sweet, milky baby puke became 'normal'.

Although the doctors and health visitors promised me it was normal, it did get to the point where I started to feel guilty. Even though it didn't bother Ivy, I was aware it was happening all the time.

For example, when she went swimming she was always sick from the movement or even laying her down on the changing mat.

Being a first time mum, also paired with anxiety really did and still does 'the dirty' to my mind. Every little thing becomes the worst case scenario in my head and then I have to act on it somehow. For example I couldn't let the reflux thing lie, just in case...

Like I always say though, the way I react is only because I care, I wouldn't want anything to happen to my little poppet and it's my job to protect her. So if it puts my mind at rest with a phone call to the doctor then what's the harm in that?

Ivy was born and spent most of her first year within the COIVD-19 Lockdown so things were a little harder when it came to making an appointment or speaking to the doctor. Luckily my health visitor understood my anxieties and put many messages through to the doctor for me. For that I am so grateful. In the end after trying many different things such as baby gaviscon and omeprazole in her bottle each morning, it was really something that got better with time.

Because the medication was not effective they then could confirm it was something to do with a little flap that doesn't close quick enough (I can't remember the name so let's call it a flap!) They told me that when she starts to sit up on her own and eat solids it will progressively get better.
 Which was so true as over time it really did get better. In fact, it just became the norm and slowly but surely it wasn't a thing anymore. Looking back my anxiety definitely got the better of me.

I guess it's our instinct to protect our children and we should never be sorry or feel silly for wanting to protect our babies.

Chapter Ten

Weaning

♥

I LOVE THIS STAGE!

Weaning is so exciting (well we found it was). Seeing your little one's face react to different textures and flavours is crazy. The only thing they've ever known is milk and each time they try something new you can see it blows their little mind!

I'll be honest I really tried to keep up with the good old Instagram mums with our weaning journey. I started by blending my own veg and freezing it with dates and even pureeing fruit to freeze. I'll admit I did turn to squeezy pouches from the supermarket occasionally, as the ones today aren't as bad as they used to be, especially for on the run because they are so quick and easy and 100% organic (i'm not saying they are just as good as fresh, so calm down mum police!). I did try as much as I could though by feeding her with what we were having, such as dinners, pasta and rice.

We never solely stuck to blended or baby led weaning, we just mixed it up depending on the food. I truly believe this is another bit of motherhood where we put so much pressure on us due to comparing ourselves to other mums and children around us. It's important to just enjoy your journey as I discovered that what other children found easy to eat, Ivy may not.

Also Ivy teethed really late so It meant she couldn't chew food like some children, so that also changed the food we could give her. It's so true when they say every child is different. It's easy for me to say now because I forever looked at other people and wondered if I was doing ok or the right thing. I guess if you're happy and so is your baby then surely it's the right thing?

I did feel fancy sometimes and make some things such as pizza swirls or broccoli tots to freeze but she soon got bored and I ended up with shit loads in my freezer, so that backfired and we just went with the flow and mixed it up each day.

She really did go through phases though, some days or even weeks she would eat very poorly and live on mini cheddars (true story) then others she would be obsessed with fruit and broccoli. This still is the case now to be honest although she is a fruit monster she will sometimes have spurts where it's really hard to get anything in her and usually we've now found that it's down to her teething or feeling off.

Which makes sense, *we* wouldn't want to eat with banging toothache or if it's 28 degrees outside either. It's easy for me to say this now but I honestly only feel (nearly two years into motherhood) I'm starting to be confident with these things.

I would forget that she is an actual human being that functions the same as us and I couldn't understand why she felt a certain way.
 I used to think it was because I was doing something wrong, then I had to tell myself she's not a robot she's

allowed to have off days!

What was always the case though (and still is), she will always eat so much more for grandparents and nursery. I swear they do it to just annoy us. How can a little human be such a trickster?! Ivy is a grazer with food, she will snack throughout the day and will ask for food when she's hungry. Although people will disagree with grazing, it works for Ivy and it means she eats. Sometimes you have to go with your 'mum instinct' as we know our child best.

The health visitors said to offer her three meals a day and if she doesn't eat it, to take it away and offer it to her again in half an hour. We still offer the meals when we sit down as a family. That wasn't and isn't the problem, she just either isn't hungry yet or doesn't eat much. That's why throughout the day she will snack on fruit, different veg, toast and yoghourts. I'm happy that she's healthy and that's all that matters. You do you, mummy! Sometimes if it's right for you, then it's right.

Chapter Eleven

Crawling

♥

Ivy was never a crawler. She was too forward in her mind and I'm sure she wanted to walk from the moment of being conceived. No but honestly, she hated the fact of trying to crawl; she rarely even attempted it. She would just lay there like a little potato, crying wanting me to move her from A to B. Which was a nightmare as we couldn't leave the room to even wee or put the washer on. I will say that stage was hard for us. She was at the point where she wanted to be on the move and not on your knee but also didn't want to crawl. In the end I think she gave up being chauffeured around the house and attempted some sort of Ivy crawl.

This *so-called* crawl consisted of both arms dragging and one leg kicking off, abit like on the side of a swimming pool. I guess she still got around though! She soon sacked that off though.

We were all at Mat's dads (Grangrans) one afternoon and he said 'Ivy are you coming with grandad whilst he makes the coffees?' Usually she would hold her hands up asking to be picked up but BOOM she trotted off following her Grandad, very fast I must say. It was typical Ivy, emotional but also comical.

This was the start of something so different and new. Although she had taken her first steps, she wasn't confident on her little legs and I guess we weren't either. So we could be hunched over holding both her hands walking

EVERYWHERE. Yes, no dragging along the floor crawling or even riding in her pushchair. The girl was on the move and she never looked back.

I will say, we love how independent she likes to be and we're super proud! Sometimes you just want to pop her in the pushchair and get from A to B but she literally screamed everytime we went to put her in, as if it was made of lava. It made it so hard for nap times or being out and about. People would stop us saying how cute she was, walking around with her big girl shoes on and I would be stood there agreeing but thinking *"no Margaret it's not cute, its back breaking and mentally challenging"*. Again, I wouldn't change her for the world, it's definitely normal to feel frustration over these little humans with tiny legs.

Chapter Twelve

Teething

♥

I'm not sure if we were classed as lucky or unlucky with teething. Ivy teethed really late, like *way* after her first birthday. Meaning we didn't have any sleepless nights due to teething whilst she was a new born, but my god it hit us hard at toddler stage.. and still is!

Our little dear gummy bear never took to a teething toy or cold teething ring, which I strongly believe may have helped cut them through and to be honest she didn't really show any signs until closer to one year old. To the point where I used to joke to Mat that she would never have teeth and we would have to take her to Turkey to have dentures!

A massive downside to teething late, is that it was affecting her eating and weaning. She struggled with certain foods, I know they say babies' gums are hard, which is true, but we still found that she couldn't manage foods like other children her age.

We went with the flow though and still gave her healthy foods, either softened, small or she just sucked it until it was nothing. As she started to get more teeth she really did surprise us because it was crazy to see what was once our little newborn, now a little girl sat watching peppa pig devouring a cheese sandwich and blueberries.

We would find ourselves just staring at her whilst she was eating because it still didn't feel right. Our baby girl was eating adult food. I know that sounds silly but I'm sure you know or will soon find out what I mean.

We also found that teething caused a whole web of symptoms for Ivy, even things you wouldn't think were connected. Yet again this caused my anxiety to be on high alert 24/7. You're probably getting the picture here that I am an anxiety riddled human being! I must say that having a baby has actually made me stronger with this though.

You wouldn't think that a sore bum like a little baboon or even a change in her bowel movements could be caused by her teggys. However, every time Ivy teethed these things would happen and we never knew if it was a bug or teething. Also she ALWAYS got a high temperature with teething as well as these symptoms so it was really hard to narrow down if it was a doctor's trip or just Calpol and bickey pegs.

I do really think our little humans are out to test us though as it really is a rollercoaster of emotions because you really want to help them but sometimes it isn't obvious what it is they need.

As she got older she would start to say *'teeth hurt'* which obviously made this ten times easier, although she became a teething powder addict and sometimes she definitely had us on. The fake cry is a huge clue. The positive thing is that we won't be having to fly her anywhere anytime soon to have some falsies fitted!

Chapter Thirteen

High temperature and febrile fits

♥

This will always be a hard thing to write, as it was an awful experience that I would never wish on anyone. Yet it also made me the mum I am today.

On Ivys first birthday she wasn't herself at all, we thought that with it being one of the hottest days of the year (as she is a July baby) it was down to her being hot and bothered or just overwhelmed with all the people at her party.

I still kick myself now that I didn't check her temperature earlier in the day but it was so hard to tell with it being so hot outside. We had fans around the house and also had to strip her down to her nappy. A close friend of mine was at the party and she said that she had noticed Ivy would push any food away after she tried to eat it, like it was hurting her when swallowing. As I watched, I saw her do it and thought the same, so I gave her some Calpol. At this point I checked her temperature but it was nothing to worry about.

In hindsight, there really was no need for a *big* birthday party for a one year old, everything was just too much. For me it was a lot of money and Ivy didn't have a clue what was happening. Don't get me wrong we made the garden look BEAUTIFUL, all woodland themed with a backdrop, balloon arch, fake leaves and of course IVY!

I went through a month or so of stress whilst planning it and I should have never pushed myself to that point because a tea party with plain paper plates would have been just as perfect. Literally a couple of days before, I came down with sinusitis a.k.a the most painful thing (other than childbirth) I have ever experienced. So as well as checking on Ivy, all the guests, keeping on top of pain relief and antibiotics for myself, the extra stress that the evening was about to bring was just the cherry on top.

So we bathed and popped Ivy to bed with no problems and then ordered a takeaway with Laura and Stew. At this point I was still obsessed with having the baby monitor right next to me (which in this case I was so grateful for). I looked at Ivy and she was curled up on her belly with her bum in the air, a way she had never slept before. I said to everyone that something didn't seem right and I wanted to go and check on her. Mat said that I was probably overthinking it but of course I could go and see. When I got to her room she was shaking so much in her sleep and was boiling to the touch.

I opened her window even wider and put her fan on max, shouting everyone to come up. We decided to bring her downstairs and give her more Calpol. Mat was on nights and reluctantly went to work. However Laura and Stew stayed with me to keep me company.

When we got her downstairs we noticed she was quite out of it, which is hard to tell when you've basically just woken them up but you get a gut feeling as a mum. Please, please mummy always go with your gut, we just know!

I took her temperature and she was 39 degrees, which shines up a bright red colour on the screen of the digital

thermometer, which gave me instant anxiety.
I rang my mum (as she just lives down the street) and asked her to come up as I could feel myself getting more anxious.

It's so hard when my anxiety starts because I pull away from the thing that's making me anxious to try and not make the situation even worse. So in situations like this I kind of go numb and struggle to deal with it. My mum arrived and laid Ivy loosely across her legs so that we didn't make her even hotter. I sat right next to them and all of a sudden I said *'why is she looking like that? Why is she now breathing like that?'*

She was motionless, like a wax work figure with her eyes glazed over. At that moment I thought I had lost her.
Suddenly her breathing started going rapidly.
Laura shouted *'quick get her in the recovery position and ring an ambulance'* At this point It was a massive emotional blur for me, I suddenly couldn't breathe and kept crying for her to be ok.
My neighbour heard the commotion coming from our house and shouted out of the window to Stew.

He explained to her that something was happening to Ivy and she said she would ring Mat to come home.

While this was happening (and waiting for the ambulance) my mum ran out the door and straight across the road to who I now call my 'superhero', although we had never spoken, we knew of her and knew she was a midwife.

The lovely lady called Kayleigh came running over in Pjs and slippers and took over the situation straight away.

By this point Ivy was 40 degrees. She explained how she thought she was having a febrile fit due to her temperature. After what felt like hours Ivy slowly came around and was just exhausted.

Mat suddenly came bursting through the door (he'd dropped everything at work) and wanted to know what had happened to his baby girl. We all cried when we saw that she was ok. I know it all seems extreme but in the moment when you don't know if she's going to be ok and what is going on, it's just a sense of relief.

Once the ambulance arrived, Ivy was up and playing, her temperature had come down massively. The ambulance crew did all her observations and confirmed that it was mostly likely a febrile fit but they wanted her to go in still to find the root cause, such as an infection.
I'll be honest, it wasn't the best experience from here.

They asked if we could take Ivy down in the car and they would let the hospital know before we got there so that they could take us straight through to paediatrics. Although I would've felt more comfortable with the ambulance crew taking her just in case it happened again, we agreed to take her in the car anyway.

My anxiety was still skyhigh at this point, and I was so scared of not knowing. Mat and I agreed it would be best if he went with in her as I wasn't in the right state of mind to support my little girl, because of covid times only one parent could go in with her. I know it sounds so awful that I didn't, but this is why Mat and I are such a good team as we understand and appreciate each other's strengths and weaknesses.

Ivy needed the parent that was going to take all the information in and be present with her. When my anxiety is at a high then nothing makes sense. I can't control my fight or flight mode and I go into complete meltdown. Like I said this is only because I care and I just want everything to be okay but I feel so out of control.

When we arrived at the hospital, I got out of the car and said to Mat *'I need to do this, I need to do it for my baby girl and be by her side'*. He supported me with this decision and told me that he would be waiting in the car if I needed to swap.

We popped her in the pram with her favourite teddy and I went to A & E with the thermometer on standby as I was so scared that at any point the temperature would spike again. I didn't know or really have a clue on how febrile fits worked and I wasn't sure if it was something that kept happening. So then I became obsessed with taking her temperature as that was the only way I could confirm if it was close to happening again. In my head it made sense.

From that moment on, that's when my anxiety got the better of me and I became obsessed with the thermometer.

I got to the A&E reception desk and explained that some information should've been sent through and we needed to be taken to paediatrics.

The receptionist booked us in and said nothing had come over from the ambulance crew and that meant we had to wait and be booked in like the other patients in A&E. I had a meltdown in front of her and asked how long the wait time was.

She advised that it was at least three hours. I said that it didn't make sense because of what the ambulance crew had said, and if I'd have known that this would've been the case then I would've demanded to go by ambulance instead of making our own way there.

I rang my auntie who is a nurse on one of the wards and cried to her, saying that I was scared and how could they leave a baby in this day and age for that long. She came straight down to A&E to comfort me and check on Ivy. She explained that if at any moment I felt Ivy was going to fit again or looked unwell then I was to shout or knock on any one of the many doors in front of me and she promised a professional would be right with me.

This is what I kept telling myself whilst battling with the thoughts that kept popping in my head. After about an hour, I couldn't bear looking at my little girl in her pram, almost lifeless but sweaty and also pale. It was so strange, she was so hot, but so pale with no flush cheeks, almost yellow looking. Eventually it got too much for me and I had to swap with Mat. When it's you or your own, it's hard to notice the other poorly people around you, but I do really believe that we should've been seen a lot sooner.

I waited in the car and tried to distract myself with the radio, but standard me kept googling instead.

The best and worst scenarios of babies and febrile fits, not making it any better at all, I know this now, but your mind is a powerful thing and I honestly think that sometimes it's very scary when you don't feel in control or connected to yourself.

As if it was normal, all of a sudden Laura pulled up next to me in the car park, she came to sit with me as she didn't want me to be alone. She sat with me until the early hours of the morning knowing she had work the next day. I will never be able to put into words how much this girl means to me and I know I may seem so over the top with my struggles but everybody has a struggle of some kind and having Ivy has highlighted that illness is a huge anxiety trigger for me.

After multiple hours sat in the car, drifting in and out of sleep and asking Laura the same question *'Is she going to be okay?'* Mat called me from the Doctors room on speaker, so I could hear for myself what he had to say. Things like this are a huge deal for me as I feel more in control when I hear things for myself. The doctor confirmed that it was indeed a febrile fit, and the root cause was tonsillitis. The infection sent Ivy's temperature skyhigh which then caused the fit.

He said to keep an eye on her temperature and give her regular doses of paracetamol and if we see the temperature starting to climb then to also add on ibuprofen. Along with the antibiotics and with a few days rest we should start to see an improvement.

We felt so relieved that there was a reason for the fit, although we wouldn't want her to have one, it was better to know that it was because of something we could treat and not something that was going to be long-term.

The next day Mat was back at work on a night shift and I was so scared to stay alone, so I decided to sleep at my mum's and have Ivy in the travel cot next to me. My mum at this point was starting to feel quite poorly and had done a Covid test, just in case.

The test came up positive with two thick, red clear lines. We all looked at each other because we knew mum and Ivy had the same symptoms which was just a little cough and temperature. It was so awful but we decided to test Ivy because around this time Covid was still really rife and many people were isolating. Her test came up straight away and it confirmed to us that she was not only trying to get over tonsillitis but Covid as well and it made so much more sense why her body reacted in the way that it did.

After a few days, she started to pick up and gradually started to eat and drink a lot more. The antibiotics were finally kicking in and our baby girl was starting to look and act a lot more like herself. A rollercoaster we would never want to ride again.

Chapter Fourteen

Holiday with a baby or toddler

♥

I'm not sure how anyone with a newborn manages to go away in this country, never mind abroad with a newborn. Honestly, if we didn't have our VW van Ivy would be sleeping in the bottom drawer with a blanket on, wearing towels for nappies and drinking from a mug.

No seriously though we stayed in Centre parks when Ivy was eight weeks old with Laura and Stew. When we started packing things into the van we soon realised how much bloody stuff we needed, or should I say wanted to take to make our lives easier.

Moses basket, beanbag chair, prep machine, steriliser, millions of nappies, clothes, bottles, pram, then all of our stuff too! If I was to have another baby and do it again, maybe I would have done it a little differently. For example maybe sterilise with hot water and milton tabs or the old fashioned way of making bottles using the kettle.

But at this point it was a scary time for us having our first holiday away. Away from all our comforts, so I guess whatever made the process less stressful and anxious we were going to do it. Also who doesn't love a little help at 2am with a prep machine that makes your bottle in about 30 seconds!

So here we are packed up to the rafters not only with our suitcases but Ivy's too and then our food on top, as we are all foodies and couldn't bare not having a hobnob with our cuppas or a cheeky camembert with some baguette just for a snack. That is us all over, so if it meant the van being slammed to the ground with weight and struggling to get over the centre parcs road humps, just for an easy, happy, holiday life. Then so be it.

When we arrived we had to let them have a look in the van to check there was no unpaid guests lurking in the back but instead they were greeted with a shitty smelling newborn, the biggest Jenga game of baby essentials and a mum and dad that needed caffeine but also both very happy to just be out the house before 11am.

I wish I could attach a photo as words just don't do it justice. Finally we had arrived though, on our first little holiday and I can honestly say it was perfect. We grew so confident as we were alone without my parents' support, with our besties and our new add on to the gang.

It was such a strange feeling, because the last time we were at Centre parcs was for our wedding as we spent the weekend there straight after saying I do!

Now instead of prosecco bottles and sexy underwear, there were baby bottles, a baby chair and a full travel system taking over the lodge. How times change!
As much as you are *the* adult, the baby is still the boss in some ways.
She demands food every two hours or more and its like the world stops turning for that.

For example, half way through a walk around the lake, there's a hot water flask, milk pods and baby bottles flying all over the place just to get baby girl fed.

At least we didn't let it stop us though, we made sure we were prepared and still went out for walks and meals. Laura and Stew as always were legends though and made the process a whole lot easier. Even if it was just Stew walking with a shitty nappy bag to the bin whilst we got sorted. We all chipped in. Even if there was shit involved.

Top tip for parents though when going out for meals. It isn't about what you would love to devour anymore, it's about what you can smash in either 3 minutes flat or what you can pick at with one hand whilst holding the baby in the other. It becomes a skill but also second nature. The first night, Mat and I ordered a half roast chicken with chips and when it came he said *'Right! Plan! You hold Ivy while I shred both chickens then it makes it easier for us, ok?'* That's teamwork right there guys, get a husband who can do both, shred chicken and hold your baby.

Your probably thinking why didn't you lay Ivy down whilst eating? That would be lovely wouldn't it and almost perfect. Unfortunately they know, I swear.

The moment you put them down with a full tummy and clean nappy and your food arrives, they remind you that they are still the most important person in the room and in fact need all the attention. At least it's the cutest attention, although all you want is to eat in peace.

You miss it weirdly, I honestly know what people mean when they say that and also when they say it goes by so quickly. That being said I would rather take any of that now, instead of playing ninja mum with cat-like reflexes at the table with my toddler. Now, If it's not cutlery that you're catching off of the table, it's skipping ads in between peppa pig videos to make the meal go more smoothly.

I would also like to say this is normal mummy, I've spent too much time worrying that Ivy was a nightmare whilst out in social situations but overtime I've spoken to many mums going through exactly the same thing.

I think all us toddler mums are also in agreement that those little colouring crayons you get with the colouring kids menu, entertain the toddler for the duration of you choosing what you want to eat. Thoughtful but useless.

Ivy loved it at centre parcs, she's always been a baby that's obsessed with the outdoors and looking at woodlands, she's always been a pram baby and a muddy puddle toddler, I never want to change that. I love that she loves the outdoors.
We would go on walks around centre parcs and she would stare at the birds and trees until she drifted off to sleep, so really it was a lot more relaxing than we anticipated.

We would then take it in turns where Mat and Stew would go off for abit and do swimming or a coffee whilst me and Laura had Ivy and then visa versa.

When Laura and I went off to do our own thing, I asked her if she could get a photo of me.

With me not long having had a baby, I'd lost my confidence and wanted to get a nice photo as the sun was out and I actually had makeup on. We found this kids race track that was for mini motos. Throughout the track there were woodland things such as giant plastic mushrooms. I shouted *'laura if stand on this will you get a photo of me?'* She said *'Well i've just sat on this one and its wobbled so are you sure its secure?'* Confidently I shout back *'yeah I'll be fine mate'*. The moment I got up on that toadstool my life flashed before my eyes! I looked up to see Laura laughing, my sunglasses were diagonal on my face and the mushroom knocked over on its side.
'I told you they weren't secure babe', Laura said softly. I just wanted to be a cool mum for a day..

The best part about it, was the moment where Mat and Stew were walking back to meet us and they just saw blonde hair whipping through the air. When we met up and I was limping with grazed knees it all made sense to them what they had witnessed from their point of view. *'I got a nice picture though'* I said under my breath looking down at my knees.

It really was a lovely holiday though and like the saying goes, we packed everything but the kitchen sink, we really did. But I honestly believe that it made the process much easier, so what if your car is packed to the rafters? If it makes your experience a whole lot easier, then go for it. You do you and if it makes you happy then perfect.

I never had to worry about how I was going to sterilise a bottle or if I was comfy enough in the lodge because we really did make it home from home. We went about our days just like we usually would only in a different setting and it was so chilled to say that we had a newborn with us and we couldn't have been happier.

It was amazing to be just us four, having chill time together with our little new addition to the gang. It really was perfect. I'm so proud of ourselves because for me it was a massive achievement. I look at people now who go out within a few days, obviously that was something that was never going to happen to me, so this was huge. I always say that I would do things differently if I was to do it again.

Who knows, if I were to do it again what would my anxiety or confidence be like? It's all a guessing game and all I can say is take it day by day and do what's right for you, as everything at some point falls into place.

Chapter Fifteen

Sleep Regression and Night terrors

So how do you get a refund? I never signed up this, finally having your baby sleep through the night to then being slapped in the face with a big fat regression. There's no inbetween either, it's 0-100 on the shock to the system scale. I am writing this chapter for you, my dear fellow mummy because I wanted to have you trained and raring to go for when this becomes a little something something.

I actually had an app that would alert me when a regression was near but I also had frequent chats with the health visitor and she would give me the heads up. Joking aside there is always the chance that your little one won't go through this and if they don't then well…I guess I'm jealous.

So basically sleep regression is when your child's sleep pattern shifts, whether it's waking in the night, struggling to fall asleep, fighting naps or genuinely forgetting what sleep is altogether. It usually happens for a couple of weeks or more and each day and night seems like a whirlwind of antics because they are so over tired that they become crazily emotional.

I can honestly say that Ivy never missed a regression, they say it is meant to happen during a developmental stage, mentally or even physically such as crawling.

Ivy was not always developing with something as obvious as that and it would be hard to pinpoint that it was a regression until either my app, health visitor or lack of sleep would alert me! There's definitely no right or wrong with how to deal with these situations.

To someone else, your way will always be the wrong way, but like I keep saying, do what is right for you. For me and Mat we were actually so laid back with how we dealt with the regressions. From three months old, Ivy slept through and in her own bed but from one year old it all changed drastically! Ivy would wake in the night screaming to come into our bed until our ears were ringing.

The way we settled her before didn't seem to work so we switched up her routine and tried many different things. We got to the point where we both agreed that she's happy and let her sleep in our bed, meaning we got enough sleep to either be a parent or work the next day.

We had many people judge us and say we were making a rod for our own back letting her in our bed, where Mat would reply *'I'm yet to meet a grown man or woman that still needs to go and get in their mum and dad's bed'*.

It's so true and still makes me giggle. Life is too short and after 4-6 months, guess what? Ivy stopped waking up to come into our bed. It just happened naturally. Now, I'm not saying it's like that for everyone, as every child is different but what I'm saying is that it works out in the end and don't beat yourself up about it because surely if your baby feels safe, then that's all that matters.

Anyway, once you have smashed one thing, another is ready and waiting around the next corner. I read something on instagram when I was first a mum. It was another mum explaining about the constant changes with baby and toddlers and she said to just be ready with a plan B. For example if they start to wake in the night, be ready with another plan such as a snack before bed, or white noise playing. I know it's not always that easy but I always had that in mind.

Our next challenge then, was Ivy waking up for a lot of milk in the night, she would usually only have one before bed but then she started becoming obsessed with wanting more. It got silly and I think for an easy life we went along with it until we knew it was time for a change up.

We started sending her to bed with a juice bottle as well and every night when she was falling to sleep we would say *'If you wake up baby, it's no more milk as your big girl juice is there for you to drink'* slowly it worked! And because her juice was in a non teat bottle, she also transitioned herself on to those bottles from teats too!

Of course, I *envied* the parents that have toddlers who sleep through without waking up but I kept telling myself it's not forever. Nowadays Ivy wakes up and we have to go back into her room until she falls back to sleep, which usually results in us falling to sleep in her bed.

We are slowly working on this and trying to go back into our own bed but as I say, sometimes you do anything if it means sleep.

The best thing is, come morning, the little two year old teennager will then be SO grumpy if you wake her up before 9. Honestly once she's in a deep sleep it's a struggle to wake her. I actually fear for when she becomes a teenager sometimes.

In between all these regressions and sleep blips, we had night terrors. Oh my lordy lord they were horrible. For us nothing we did would calm Ivy down; she would scream and cry but would appear as if she was awake. She would usually want to get out of the room where she'd had the night terror because she would be so scared to be in that room.

It happened once when we were on holiday in Spain and the hotel walls were super thin. My Nannie ended up coming to help us calm her down as she couldn't ignore how distressed she sounded. We ended up opening the balcony doors to let a draft in to try and snap her out of it.

Many people said things, such as don't wake them but it was always hard to tell because she came across as if she was awake, just very distressed.

When it would happen at home we would usually bring her downstairs for 10 minutes, to try and take her mind off it but not a lot helped. She would usually calm down when she saw something that she wanted, such as a teddy or a random object like a drinks coaster haha! Honestly she could go to bed with a garden brush if it meant calming her down!

We realised it happened the most when she was over tired like on holiday, we would miss naps with her being too excited, or at home if she went to bed later than usual.

Slowly she grew out of constantly having them and we made an effort of keeping a routine for her. Obviously the odd time for special occasions would slightly change. So if this happens to you, don't worry, your child isn't possessed, it's most likely a night terror and they 100% will not mutate into some green eyed monster. At least that hasn't happened for us yet.

Chapter Sixteen

First Birthday party and the future

♥

My friend once said to me, *'just some words of advice, don't go all out for Ivy's first birthday, she won't remember it and it's a lot of money.'* I looked at her with tumble weeds behind my eyes and agreed. Then in my head I thought *'if only you knew my plan'* I didn't listen. I went for it, I couldn't not. All woodland themed with Ivy's name tying in.

Looking back, was she right? Hell yes. As soon as the party was over I said to Mat *'am I frig doing this again next year'*. I don't regret the party at all as everyone that came enjoyed it so it wasn't a waste but it opened my eyes to how much effort you can put into something and the money. Yet if it was in my living room with cocktail sausages they would have enjoyed it just the same. The balloon arch I stressed about getting up at the last minute or the party bags I had homemade cookies in, really didn't matter. It looked absolutely beautiful don't get me wrong and when I look at the photos I am so proud, but Ivy really had no clue.

If anything because Ivy ended up being ill and having a fit, I almost felt deflated and maybe that's why I have a bad feeling towards the party.

Either way I truly think I didn't need all the decorations and food. Me and Mat couldn't enjoy it like all the family were as we were running around doing the obvious.

Checking everyone had drinks, enough food, that the kids all had sun cream on and basically just entertaining. For the family it was a lovely get together in the sun with free food and drink.

I mean you don't know stress until it's the hottest day of the year and you have egg and tuna sandwiches in the kitchen and only one table top fan to try and cool the room down, it was like a gnat blowing on a buffet.

When her second birthday came around, we agreed a party wasn't worth it and we would take her out for the day instead. We took her to one of her favourite places called sundown, she ran riot for the day doing things that she loved. We then came home and had cake, just with us and she was so happy, she really did have the best time and it was a fraction of the cost of her first birthday. In the pictures her first birthday looked amazing but Ivy looks so fed up with people holding her, she just wanted to be a toddler and run around, which she definitely got to do this time round.

Don't get me wrong I'm not saying big badass parties should be illegal that might be perfect for you but for me I'm definitely learning as I go and I would rather do what's right for us, happy family happy life.
I just want her to feel loved and special each birthday.

Obviously I want her to feel that all the time but growing up, your birthdays are magical and you count down the days for months before. I want her to know that it's her day and it matters. Growing up, my birth dad has been hot and cold and in and out my life all the time.

Some birthdays it would be a card in the post, some he would visit and others it would be a meal. I never knew where I stood, to be honest it made me get a little anxious for my birthdays, it was always the not knowing. Now I have my own little mini me, I know which feelings matter and I always want her to feel them.

To me she is the most important thing that walks this earth and whilst I am on this earth she will feel it. Some may say 'spoiled' but to me it's how your parents should make you feel. I am and always will be Ivy's number one biggest fan and if it means me watching random YouTube videos with her on her birthday morning with breakfast then lovely, because my girl is happy.

I guess what I'm trying to say is that it's about love and how your child feels. If they are happy playing with play dough for the day in their pants on their birthday then surely that's perfect. That's what they will remember, they were able to do what they chose on their birthday.

I remember birthdays differently. I also remember the effort my mum put in even though she was poorly, I always blew candles out on a cake whether it was handmade or Colin the caterpillar. She knew that mattered. For a young child a cake matters as that is what you associate birthdays with.

Throwing crazy party's to me doesn't always show love and affection but quality time and the understanding of what makes you happy does. I hope that makes sense..

Ah the future, I still haven't got full control of this 'mum thing' and I'm doubting myself everyday but I feel that making my own mistakes and creating my own memories is only making me stronger. I will never say I have found it easy, in fact everyday I feel like I'm waking up in an episode of I'm a celebrity each day, as I don't know what's going to happen next.

What I can say though, is no matter what each day brings it always has at least one smile or laugh, especially with a toddler. That makes up for everything. I couldn't imagine my life any different now, I would be well and truly bored, as she sure does keep me on my toes. I'm excited for the future as we have so much to achieve and experience together.

If it wasn't for becoming a mum then I wouldn't have come this far. Ivy has turned my world upside down and added sunshine in a crazy way. It's because of her that I'm writing this book, even if it helps just one parent then I'm happy. It's a crazy whirlwind and it's about not feeling alone and also knowing it's ok to feel these raw feelings sometimes.

On the flip side if you can find me someone that's not expecericed any of these things then please give them the biggest pat on the back because evidently they are a fucking genius.

Dear my sweet girl Ivy,

Im not sure if you will ever read this book, but if you don't, I will make sure you at least read this letter. I need you to know how you turned my world upside down for the better.

I always struggled with my anxiety and found it hard when I had to spend time alone. When I was 10 weeks pregnant with you I went to have a facial massage and as I lay with the tranquil music in the background (which probably didn't help and the pregnancy hormones on top) a sudden rush of emotion, good emotion, came over me. I didn't feel alone anymore, because I wasn't, I had you. From then on I would never be alone on the good and bad days, I had you. My little best friend.

I know this book speaks majorly about how I

struggled at the start becoming your mummy, but I promise you that was never your fault. That was motherhood testing me and me growing as a mummy. If it wasn't for you I wouldn't have grown and experienced new things. You gave me confidence I never knew I had. I have achieved so much more in the two years of having you than I ever have in my life time, because of YOU.

I thank my lucky stars every day for being blesssed with you in my life and our little love bubble is the most important thing to me in the world. I wish for our lives to be filled with the best memories together and I will help you achieve and be confident just like you have me.

The world can be a scary place but remember you are never alone, no matter what happens or is thrown at you in life. You can always find love and strength with your mummy and daddy.

You are an amazing, funny, crazy little girl and I want you to shine forever.

Love Mummy
Your forever best friend x

A little Thankyou

Lastly I could not finish this book without saying a HUGE thank you to my lovely friend Stew.
From late night editing with you with endless cup of teas and sweet treats we created together everything that I imagined.

Not only have you always been by mine and Mats side throughout every journey of ours, you have also helped make something so important to me happen.

Love you Babi! X

Next my friends and family that have helped me grow so much as a person over the last three years, I would not be where I am now without all your constant support and love. Im truly blessed with the most amazing family and friends.

Then my Team, Mathew and Ivy.
MY ABSOLUTE WORLD AND MORE

Without you two I wouldn't have this story to tell and I feel the luckiest girly in the world.
All I wish for is to wake up each day in our lovely home with you two lovely human beings. You both are my sunshine on a rainy day. xxx

Printed in Great Britain
by Amazon